Lettering and Liking it Too!

Hundreds of fun and creative ways to add more _spark_ and _style_ to your lettering projects!

Designed by Sandra O. Tyson

Published by Wasatch Mountain Design

P. O. Box 70171 Salt Lake City, UT 84170-0171

(801) 969-1808

Copyright ©1997 WMD

"50 WAYS TO

Everywhere you look you see letters expressed in so many different ways! Each expresses its own personality and style. There are thousands of ways to express feelings and attitudes by the way letters are shaped!

LETTERS LETTERS

2

"Leave Your Letters"

LETTERS LETTERS

Letters LETTERS Letters

letters LETTERS LETTERS

LETTERS LETTERS LETTERS

Letters LETTERS Letters

letters LETTERS

LETTERS letters Letters

LETTERS Letters

LETTERS LETTERS LETTERS

LETTERS letters

LETTERS Letters

LETTERS LETTERS

©WMD 1997

3

Change your Pen--- ---Change your Look

ABCDEFGHIJKLM
NOPQRSTUVWXYZ

·fine point tip·

ABCDEFGHIJKLM
NOPQRSTUVWXYZ

·medium point tip·

ABCDEFGHIJKLM
NOPQRSTUVWXYZ

·bullet tip·

ABCDEFGHIJKLM
NOPQRSTUVWXYZ

·small calligraphy tip·

The alphabets on these 2 pages are exactly the same. The only difference is the pen tip that was used to write them! You can see how different each one looks by just changing pens! If you are stuck in the "same pen rut", try some of these other great pen tips!

ABCDEFGHIJKLM
NOPQRSTUVWXYZ

· large calligraphy tip--held horizontally ·

ABCDEFGHIJKLM
NOPQRSTUVWXYZ

· large calligraphy tip--held vertically ·

ABCDEFGHIJKLM
NOPQRSTUVWXYZ

· scroll tip ·

ABCDEFGHIJKLM
NOPQRSTUVWXYZ

· brush tip ·

Simple...or...Splashy!

narrow tips do it all!

Fun in the Sun!

rub-a-dub-dub

Welcome to the world, little one!

DRILL TEAM

land of the free, home of the brave...

Jr. High

HAPPY, HAPPY DAY!

PICTURE PERFECT... 1234567 890

abcdefghijk lmnopqrstuvwxyz

©WMD 1997

Ouch! rah!

Hand over your CHOCOLATE AND no one GETS hurt!

I Love Kids!

U S A

TOO MUCH FUN!

Summer FUN!

1 2 3 4 5 6 7 8 9 0

A b C d E f G h i j K l m N O P q R s T u V w x Y z

GIVE BULLET TIPS

a B C D e f G h I J k L m n
O P Q R S t U V W X y Z

Bullet tips are wonderful for alphabets with a classic, clean look—

1 2 3
4 5 6
7 8 9

A B C D E F G H I J K L M N O
P Q R S T U V W X Y Z

A bullet tip gives a nice rounded end to each stroke.

A B C D E F G H I J K L M N O P
Q R S T U V W X Y Z
1 2 3 4 5 6 7 8 9 0

A BABY GIRL!

A SHOT!

Bullet tip pens are great for a bold look! They are super for titles and larger letters!

HOLLYWOOD

—Here I come!—

'Atta Boy!

IT'S SPRING!

WOW!

ABCDEF
GHIJKLM
NOPQRST
UVWXYZ

©WMD 1997

FANTASTIC!

9

CALLIGRAPHY TIP

ABCDEFG
HIJKLMNO
PQRSTUV
WXYZ

"Top Heavy" alphabet with tip at horizontal.

DANCE!

HAPPY
BIRTHDAY

ADIOS

Calligraphy tip pens are no longer only for those who know calligraphy! There are so MANY great looks you can get by using various sizes of calligraphy tips. Try changing the angle of the tip from vertical to horizontal, and anything in between! Try these examples to see if you can tell how the pen was used to achieve each look.

ABCDEF
GHIJKL
MMNOP
QRSTU
VWXYZ

Full width of tip used for thick lines; corner of pen used for thin lines.

abcdefghijklmn op

Mixed capital & lower case alphabet with tip at horizontal.

QRSTUVWXYZ

10

©WMD 1997

HALLOWEEN

Try this great looking one! It takes a little concentration at first, but you'll pick it up quickly! Every stroke is done with the full pen width. You must turn the pen in your hand to do each stroke, and continue to turn your hand as the lines curve. Pick up the pen as needed to reposition the angle of the tip.

AB
CD
EF
GH
IJ
KL
MN
OP

QR
ST
UV
WX
YZ

Scott

Don't forget the great borders calligraphy tips can make!

©WMD 1997

Perhaps you have shied away from trying a scroll tip pen because you weren't sure what to do with it? Scroll tips are so fun! You just handle them in exactly the same way you would a calligraphy pen!

scroll tip~

ABCDEFGHIJ
KLMNOPQ
RSTUVWXYZ

abcde
fghijkl
mnopq
rstu
vwxyz!!

For this alphabet, the pen was held at about 45°.

1234567890

tip: If you are new to a scroll tip pen and get confused by the double lines as you write, concentrate your focus on one line only— the lower one, and ignore the other.

= =

Celebrate~!

I love you
SQUARE
WOW!

A scroll tip creates a "shadow" automatically. It is important to keep your pen held very vertically in your hand to make sure both sides of the tip are contacting the page. Your letter ends can be left "open" or you can close them using the corner of the pen. Look at these examples of open & closed ends, and see if you can tell at what angle the tip was held.

under construction

"two, two, two tips in one!"

USE YOUR SCROLL TIP FOR FORMAL OR INFORMAL LOOKS!

ANNOUNCING:

ABC DEF

MAN OF THE YEAR!

congrats!

OUR TRIP TO MEXICO

double date

Experiment with a scroll tip on your borders!

One advantage a scroll tip has over a calligraphy tip is the space in between the lines! Fill in the space with other colors or designs!

Hawaii

Cursive looks great with a scroll tip—

~Recital~

fill in

©WMD 1997

13

brush tip

A brush tip pen is great for casual, free flowing alphabet styles !
With the flexible tip, you can get very fine or very bold lines,
depending on the amount of pressure you put on the tip.

A brush tip pen is held differently than other pens. Most of the strokes
are made with the side of the brush, so you need to hold the pen more
horizontally in your hand. Try holding the pen nearer to the brush than
you do with your other pens. You will get a quicker response from the
tip as you release the pressure on the tip for your fine lines.

abcdefghijklmn

opqrstuvwxyz

Script

abcdefghijklmnopq

rstuvwxyz

Welcome

The End

happy holidays

THE DESERT

Great for filling in block letters or scroll tip letters!

DOUBLE TROUBLE

Kindergarten

Just for fun!
Use your brush tip pen with your stencils or templates! Fill in solid or try this fun "scribble" style! It's so easy! Brush tips are super for free hand drawing too!

A B C D E F G H I J K L M N O P Q R S T U W X Y Z

©WMD 1997

15

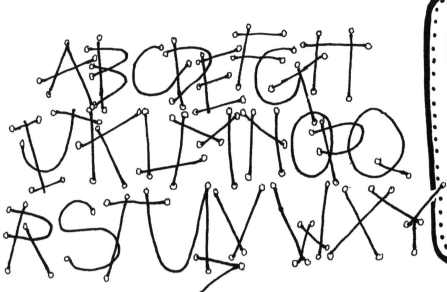

ABCDEFGHIJKLMNOPQRSTUVWXYZ

More Fun With Old Favorites!
· DOTS · Serifs · Deco ·

HAPPY NEW YEAR!

tennis, anyone!

you should be dancin'...

WELCOME FRIENDS

families are ♥ forever

ABCDEFGHIJKLM
NOPQRSTUVWXYZ

© WMD 1997

ABCD
EFGH
JKLM
NOPQR
STUVW
XYZ

nitey-night

AMIE

FOREVER YOUNG!

ABCD
EFGH
IJKL
MNOP
QRSTUV
WXYZ

AFRICA

Happy Holidays

ANDREA

YELLOWSTONE

ANGLES

ABCDEFGHIJKLM
NOPQRSTUVWXYZ

Change the look
of your words
with angles and curls !
Get formal, fancy or
funky !

ROCK 'N' ROLL

ASHLEY

Little Devin's
Big Fish!

TRICK OR TREAT!

CALVIN BOY SCOUTS

1234567890

ABCDEFGHIJKLM
NOPQRSTUVWXYZ

& Curls ~

A B C D E F
G H I J K
L M N O P Q
R S T U V
W X Y Z

a b c d e f g h i j k l m
n o p q r s t u v w
x y z

My
Glassroom

1 2 3 4 5
6 7 8 9 0

JOSIE

a b c d e f
g h i j k
l m n o
p q r s t u
v w x y z

BABY
BABY

A B C D E
F G H I J K
L M N O P
Q R S T U V
W X Y Z

©WMD 1997

19

JOY

Aa Bb Cc Dd
Ee Ff Gg Hh Ii
Jj Kk Ll Mm Nn Oo Pp
Qq Rr Ss Tt Uu
Vv Ww Xx Yy Zz

1 2 3 4 5 6 7 8 9

gone fi shun →

give thanks

Our Cabin

SUNFLOWERS

"the good old days"

© WMD 1997

Warm Thoughts, Happy Memories

I LOVE YOU.

"HARVEST TIME"

live well, laugh often, love much

Our Family history

WELCOME HOME

Merry Christmas

HOME SWEET HOME

grandma and grandpa

©WMD 1997

BLOCK LETTERS
the Possibilities are endless!

Block letters are perhaps the most versatile of all! There are so many fun things to do with them! The next few pages show some of the many variations. If you are new to block letters, write your word in pencil first, then outline around the lines to get the shape you want! Let your imagination go!

SEAN

SURF'S UP!

HIGH SCHOOL

NICK

OLIVIA

HOORAY!

MATT

SENIOR YEAR!

cursive

spring!

22

©WMD 1997

feelin' groovy

Memories...

PEACE

LOVE Ya!

ABCDEFG HIJKLM NOPQRS TUVWXYZ

abcdefgh ijklmnopqr stuvwxyz

have a nice day!

©WMD 1997

23

Wild, Wacky,

ABCDE
FGHiJKL
MNOPQ
RSTUV
WXYZ

LITTLE
RASCALS

1 2 3
4 5 6 7
8 9 0 & My favorites:

GNARLY DUDE!

PARTY!

AWESOME!

© WMD 1997

SUPER KID!

WARPED, WEIRD!

CONGRATULATIONS!

FUN IN THE SUN!

Slumber Party!

LINDSAY

LOOK AT THIS!

the ZOO!

©WMD 1997

Shading...

The principle of shading assumes that there is a light source shining on the letters which casts a shadow from them. The sun at the top of this page is 'shining' on the word to the left. The shadow is cast on the right and bottom surfaces of the letters. The same principle applies no matter where the light source is coming from— a shadow is cast on the surfaces opposite from where the light is shining. The examples below show how the shading would look when the light shines from different angles.

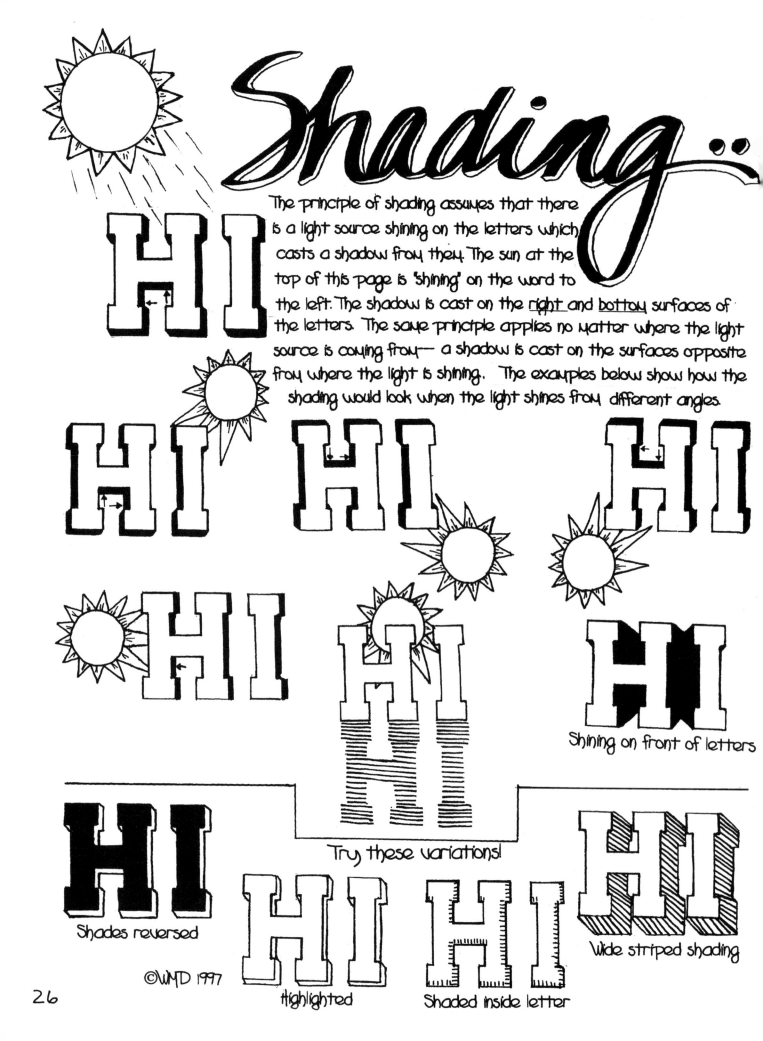

Shining on front of letters

Try these variations!

Shades reversed

Highlighted

Shaded inside letter

Wide striped shading

©WMD 1997

26

gives DIMENSION

Shading adds More "oomph" to your letters, giving them a "3-D" look !

SCHOOL IS COOL!

MAYA

OLÉ

ALEX the GREAT

CARMEN

PROM NIGHT

SUMMER

REVERSE

Draw block letters in pencil first, do shading and then erase pencil !

©WMD 1997

JAZZ BAND

BEYOND BASIC BLOCKS:

Take your block letters a little further by using this fun technique! All of the examples shown here are done with the same principle : First, write your block letter word in pencil. Second, with your pen draw in the additions (or subtractions in some cases!) to the letters.(See 'snow' letters below.) Third, fill in the rest of the letter with your pen and erase any pencil lines. It's so easy!! (and that's no 'snow job !")

1. WINTER

2. WINTER

3. WINTER

WET PAINT!

ICE COLD

FLOWERS

VOLCANO

heat!

28

RAINY DAY

SWIM

SNOWY

HOT!

WIND

AWESOME

CHEESE

MOUNTAIN

SUMMER

SKIING

©WMD 1997

29

More Fun With Blocks!

Use your stencils and templates to create "blocks" for your letters to fit inside of! Just rotate the shape as you trace each one. Or, freehand your blocks for a more casual look! Then fill in with whatever you like!

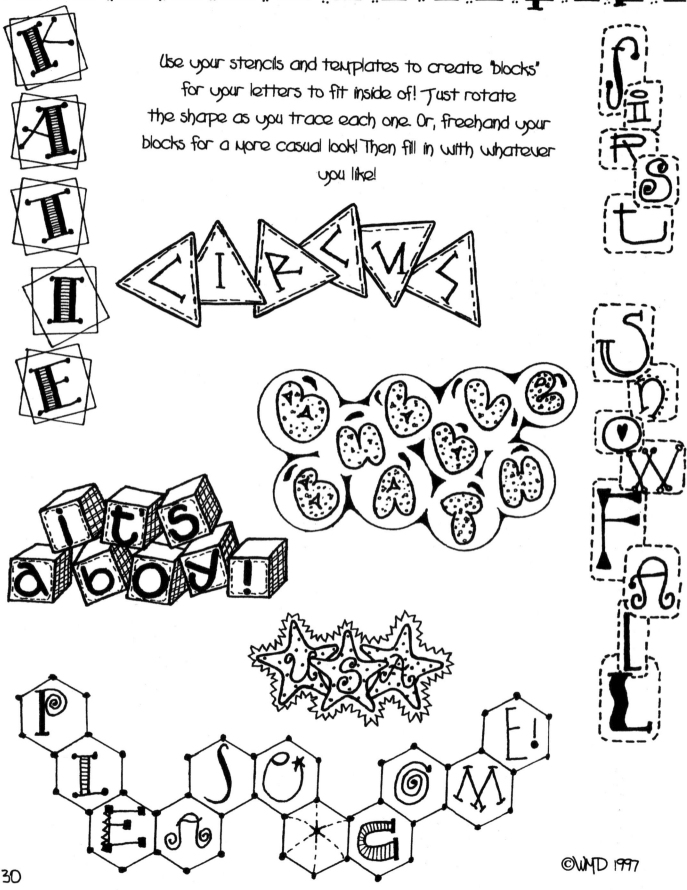

KATIE

FIRST SNOWFALL

CIRCUS

BABY GIRL BATH

it's a boy!

USA

PLEASE COME!

More than Words...

The idea of adding art to words was introduced in <u>Lettering & Liking It!</u>, showing how adding a sketch or drawing to a title can add so much to its "personality!" You don't need to be an artist to add simple designs—just use your imagination! It's so fun that once you get started you'll keep thinking of more things you can do! Give it a try!

AHOY

Home is where your Honey is!

POOL

It Was This Big!

EARTH SHATTERING!

Together forever

VACATION

©WMD 1997

31

OUR DAD!

HAPPY BIRTHDAY!

Beach

WE'VE MOVED!
1148 VINE ST.
FRESNO,
CALIFORNIA

4 JULY

VOTE

HO HO HO

32

© WMD 1997

DAD'S DAY!

SNOW

...You are my sunshine, my only sunshine, you'll never know dear, how much I love you, please don't take my sunshine away. Happy

STARRING:

magical

LOVE

Merry Christmas

©WMD 1997

33

DISNEY LAND '96
Susan Grant
Springville, UT

Across
People are

The following pages are the fun ideas shared by readers around the country!

MERRY CHRISTMAS
Kimberly Parkin
Riverton, UT

Swim lessons
Susan Grant
Springville, UT

Golf
Annette Mills
Pleasant Grove, UT

finger licking good
Susan Grant
Springville, UT

the Miles...
lettering & liking it!

Thanks for the "Miles of Ideas!"

THE HONEYMOON

Sherry Mills
Torrance, CA

ALCATRAZ

Sherry Mills
Torrance, CA

PARK

Shay Moore
Richmond, IN

CHICKEN POX

Deonne Lindberg
age 14
American Fork, UT

piano

Fran Grossenbacher
Gilbert, AZ

MEOW

Kimberly Parkin
Riverton, UT

Batter Up!

Fran Grossenbacher
Gilbert, AZ

35

GUITAR

Lynne Whitaker
Buena Park, CA

Lynne Whitaker
Buena Park, CA

GYM

BASEBALL

Lynne Whitaker
Buena Park, CA

Delta Chi

The Beach

Michelle Lacy
Centerville, UT

Michelle Lacy
Centerville, UT

Michelle Lacy
36 Centerville, UT

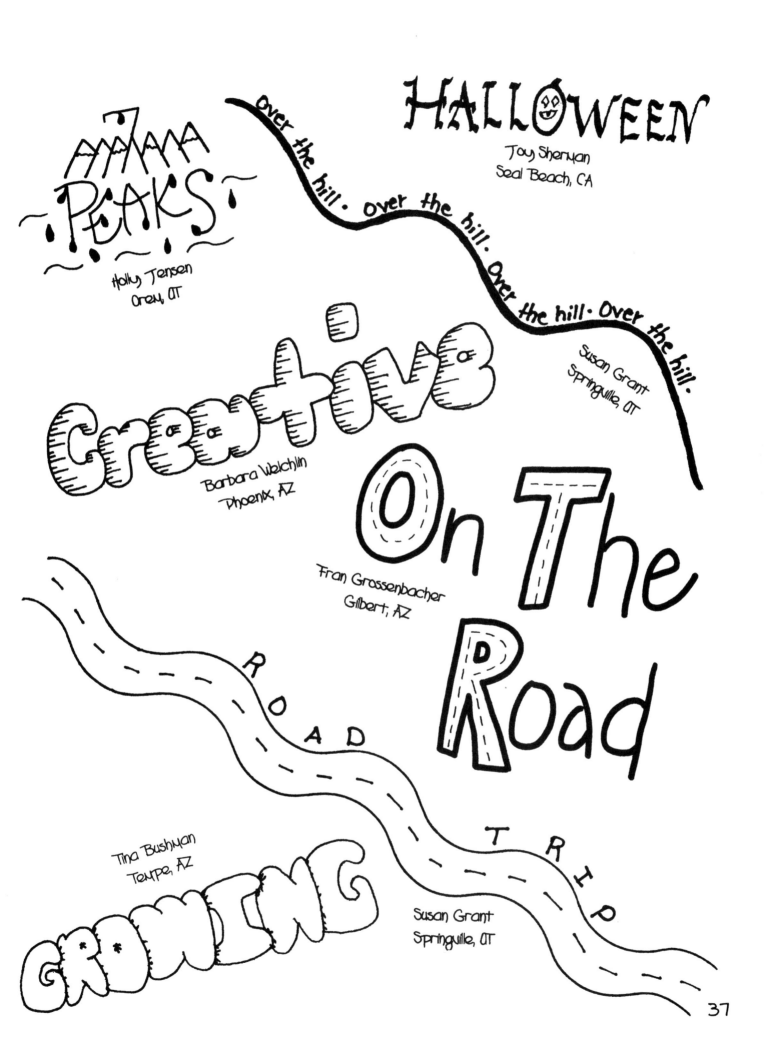

PEAKS
Holly Jensen
Orem, UT

Over the hill · Over the hill · Over the hill · Over the hill.
Susan Grant
Springville, UT

HALLOWEEN
Joy Sherman
Seal Beach, CA

Creative
Barbara Welchlin
Phoenix, AZ

On The Road
Fran Grossenbacher
Gilbert, AZ

ROAD TRIP
Susan Grant
Springville, UT

GROWING
Tina Bushman
Tempe, AZ

37

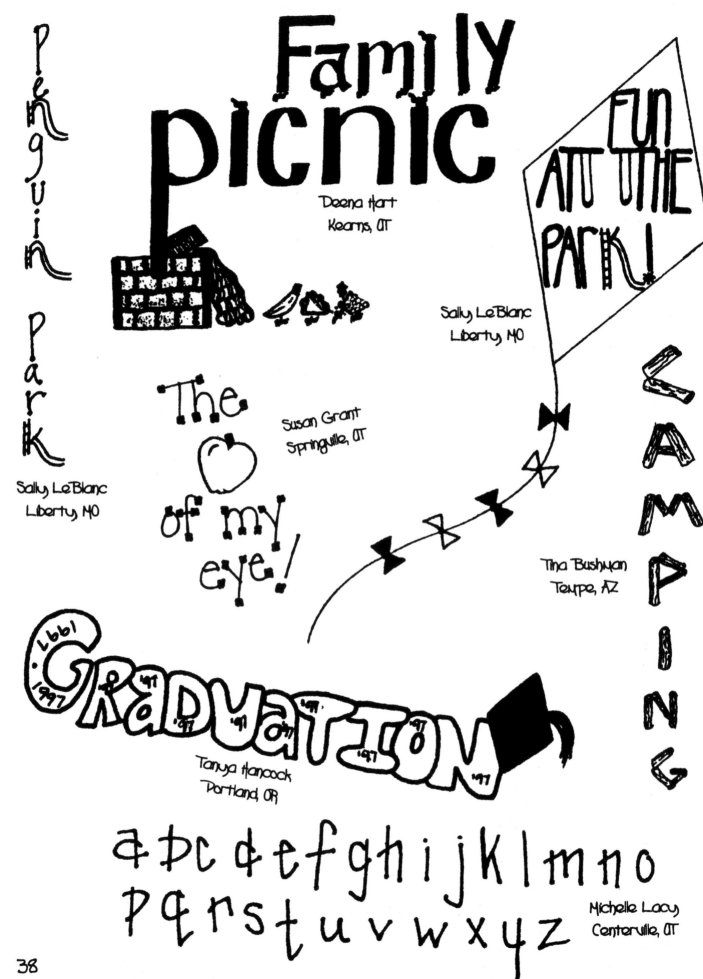

Penguin Park

Family picnic
Deena Hart
Kearns, UT

Sally LeBlanc
Liberty, MO

Fun at the Park!
Sally LeBlanc
Liberty, MO

The ♥ of my eye!
Susan Grant
Springville, UT

Camping
Tina Bushman
Tempe, AZ

Graduation 1997
Tanya Hancock
Portland, OR

a b c d e f g h i j k l m n o p q r s t u v w x y z
Michelle Lacy
Centerville, UT

California
Tina Bushman
Tempe, AZ

FISHING WITH DAD
Tanya Hancock
Portland, OR

ISRAEL
anonymous
Danville, CA

_____ Dayton
Orem, UT

WHEELER FARM
Susan Grant
Springville, UT

Arizona
Fran Grossenbacher
Gilbert, AZ

Karma Wood
Logan, UT

Shadow

39

Watch Me Grow

1 2 3 4 5 6 7 8

Susan Grant
Springville, UT

GET WELL
happy pill
ACE

Deonne Lindberg
age 14
American Fork, UT

Susan Grant
Springville, UT

I wanna be a cowboy

Oink

Susan Grant
Springville, UT

BACK TO SCHOOL

Tina Bushman
Tempe, AZ

beach

Fran Grossenbacher
Gilbert, AZ

PICNIC

HOT TIMES

Esther Middleton
Mesa, AZ

Tanya Hancock
Portland, OR

40